*Countries Around the World*
# Mexico

Ali Brownlie Bojang

Chicago, Illinois

**www.heinemannraintree.com**
Visit our website to find out more information about Heinemann-Raintree books.

**To order:**
☎ Phone 888-454-2279
🖳 Visit www.heinemannraintree.com to browse our catalog and order online.

Edited by Louise Galpine and Megan Cotugno
Designed by Ryan Frieson
Original illustrations © Capstone Global Library, Ltd.
Illustrated by Oxford Designers & Illustrators
Picture research by Tracy Cummins
Originated by Capstone Global Library, Ltd.
Printed in China by China Translation and Printing Services

15 14 13 12
10 9 8 7 6 5 4 3 2

Library of Congress Cataloging-in-Publication Data
Brownlie Bojang, Ali, 1949-

  Mexico / Ali Brownlie Bojang.
     p. cm.—(Countries around the world)
  Includes bibliographical references and index.
  ISBN 978-1-4329-5213-6 (hc)—ISBN 978-1-4329-5238-9 (pb)
1. Mexico. I. Title.
  F1208.B85 2012
  972—dc22                    2010043251

**Acknowledgments**

The author and publishers are grateful to the following for permission to reproduce copyright material: © AP Photo: pp. 17 (© Guillermo Arias), 37 (© Eduardo Verdugo); © Corbis: p. 11 (© CORBIS); © Getty Images: pp. 13 (Frank Scherschel//Time Life Pictures), 16 (Ronaldo Schemidt/AFP/), 19 (JANET SCHWARTZ/AFP), 20 (George Lepp), 25 (Joe Raedle/Newsmakers), 28 (John & Lisa Merrill), 33 (Steve Peixotto), 35 (Frans Lemmens); © istockphoto: pp. 14 (© Alexandra Draghici), 46 (© Dieter Spears); © Library of Congress Prints and Photographs Division: p. 23; © Photolibrary: pp. 26 (Mark Edwards), 30 (Tim Hill); © Shutterstock: pp. 5 (© Thomas Cristofoletti), 6 (© Brian Chase), 7 (© Yvan), 9 (© gary yim), 12 (© csp), 18 (© Ewan Chesser), 21 (© douglas knight), 29 (© CHRISTIAN ARAUJO), 39 (© Elena Elisseeva).

Cover photograph reproduced with permission of Getty Images (Kim Steele).

We would like to thank Sarah Blue for her invaluable help in the preparation of this book.

# Contents

Some words in the book are in bold, **like this**. You can find out what they mean by looking in the glossary.

# Introducing Mexico

When you think of Mexico, many pictures and sounds may come into your mind. You may think first of beautiful beaches, spicy food, and cacti. Maybe you have visited Mexico and know that most people there speak Spanish and that there is a special day to celebrate the dead! In this book, you will learn many more fascinating facts about Mexico.

Mexico is a vast country of nearly 2 million square kilometers (772,204 square miles). It's the 15th largest country in the world and is about three times the size of Texas. Mexico lies between the United States and Central America. It is north of the Equator. There are many different peoples and landscapes in Mexico, and its history dates back thousands of years.

## Mexico today

Mexico has the largest Spanish-speaking population in the world. Also, over 60 traditional languages are still spoken. Nearly 80 percent of the people live in large towns and cities. Most live a modern lifestyle that would be familiar to people in any developed country. But in some of the more remote villages, life continues in ways that have not changed for hundreds of years.

### *How to say...*

*Hola* means "hello" in Spanish. You pronounce it oh-la. Many words in English have Spanish origins, such as *cafeteria* (cafeteria), *barbacoa* (barbecue), *cucaracha* (cockroach), *tomate* (tomato), *vainilla* (vanilla), and *huracán* (**hurricane**).

Cacti are typical of the
desert areas of Mexico.

# History: Civilizations, Conquest, and Struggle

Mexico's history goes back thousands of years. It has been the home of magnificent **civilizations**. It has been invaded and conquered. It has struggled for its independence. Its population of over 111 million is descended from the different people who have been part of its history. The first Mexicans were probably descended from people who arrived from Asia over 10,000 years ago. They crossed the frozen Bering Sea between Russia and Alaska during the Ice Age.

## The age of civilizations

About 3,000 years ago, the Olmec, Zapotec and the Mayan civilizations were established. The Mayans built palaces, temples, and observatories to record the sun's movement across the sky. They also developed a system of writing.

Over 600 years ago, the Aztecs, another great Mexican civilization, settled in Mexico and conquered lands and people. They were an advanced and orderly people, but their warriors were fierce and violent. The Aztecs believed that human sacrifice was needed for their society to survive. Like the Mayans, the Aztecs built palaces, temples, and pyramids. The descendants of the early peoples of these early civilizations make up 30 percent of Mexico's population.

Mexico gave chocolate to the world. The Aztecs called it *xocóatl*, which means "bitter water."

## Daily Life

Mexico City is built over the Aztec city of Tenochtitlán. It is on a high **plateau** with thin air. This is surrounded by mountains, which trap the traffic and factory exhaust fumes. It is not a healthy place to live. Many people who live there suffer from serious breathing problems.

Early Mexican peoples left behind many clues to their advanced civilizations.

## The Spanish conquest

The Aztec Empire was destroyed in 1521 when the Spanish **conquistador** Hernán Cortés and his army invaded Mexico. The conquistadors were Spanish explorers and adventurers. They had heard stories of gold and silver in Mexico and sailed across the Atlantic Ocean in search of their fortunes.

## Life under the Spanish

Mexico became a Spanish **colony**. Many thousands of Aztecs and other native peoples were killed during and after the invasion. The Europeans also brought infectious diseases with them, to which these peoples had no resistance. Thousands died of diseases, such as measles and **typhus**.

The Spanish rulers treated the native population very badly. They were forced to work as slaves on farms and down mines, and were not allowed to have a say in how the country was run. The Spanish destroyed many impressive native structures.

## Independence

After 300 years of Spanish rule, in 1810 Mexican-born Spaniards, *mestizos*, and native peoples rebelled and fought against the Spanish colonial rulers. Thousands of people were killed in the war that followed. Mexico finally became independent in 1821. While this new freedom benefited some people, most of the population continued to be very poor.

### MOCTEZUMA II (C.1470–1520)

Moctezuma II was the Aztec ruler at the time of the Spanish conquest. He welcomed the Spanish and gave them gifts. But Cortés had him arrested and then eventually murdered.

## How to say...

The word "Mexico" comes from *Mexica* (pronounced Me-shee-ka), the name sometimes given to the Aztecs.

The city of Guanajuato is a **UNESCO World Heritage site**. The cathedral is built in the Spanish style.

## The Mexican Revolution

After independence, Mexico's wealth remained in the hands of just a few rich people. They continued to take land from the poor, and developed large **plantations**, or *haciendas*. They grew sugar, rice, and coffee to sell abroad. Unrest among the poor led to the outbreak of **civil war** in 1910. A rebellion was led by Francisco Madero against the rule of the **dictator** Porfirio Diaz, who represented the rich. The fighting lasted for ten years, and about two million people were killed. The revolution finally succeeded and a new Revolutionary Party was formed, which brought in changes to help the poor, such as **land redistribution** and more rights for workers.

## World War II

During World War II, after German submarines attacked Mexican ships, Mexico became an **ally** of the United States and Britain. In fact, only the Mexican Air Force fought, but other Mexicans flocked across the border into the United States to help support the war effort.

## Recent history

For 71 years, one political party, the Institutional Revolutionary Party (PRI), won every presidential race and controlled Mexico's national government. Many people thought that they succeeded by cheating. In July 2000, Vicente Fox Quesada, of a different political party—the National Action Party (PAN)—was elected. These elections were thought to be the freest and fairest in Mexican history.

### EMILIANO ZAPATA (C. 1877–1919)

Emiliano Zapata grew up in a poor peasant family of mixed native peoples and Spanish ancestry—a *mestizo*. He formed the Liberation Army of the South during the Mexican Revolution. His followers were known as *Zapatistas*. Today he is a national hero.

Many women fought in the Mexican Revolution.

# Regions and Resources: A Land of Variety

Mexico is part of North America. The **Tropic of Cancer** cuts through the middle of the country. Mexico is one of only two countries that shares a border with the United States—the other is Canada. Mexico has borders in the south with Guatemala and Belize. The Pacific Ocean is to the west of Mexico and the Gulf of Mexico to the east.

## A fiery, shaking land

Three large **tectonic plates** meet beneath Mexico. These are enormous areas of Earth's crust that fit together like a giant puzzle. They move very slowly, but sometimes pressure builds up and they move with a jolt, causing earthquakes and volcanoes. The earthquakes in turn can cause **tsunamis**.

Baja California is the second longest **peninsula** in the world.

# Daily Life

In 2000 nearly 56,000 people living near the Popocatepeti volcano were told to leave their homes as the volcano erupted. It sent showers of red-hot rocks hundreds of feet into the night sky. There were huge traffic jams as people escaped to temporary shelters.

Mount Paricutin erupted in 1943, burying buildings and people.

Many of Mexico's volcanoes are **extinct**, but there are seven major **active** volcanoes. Mount Paricutin is one of the newest volcanoes in the world. In 1943 a fissure, or crack, appeared in a farmer's cornfield. Ash and stones erupted through the crack and within a week it had formed a hill as high as a large building. Today it is 424 meters (1,391 feet) high.

Mexico has frequent earthquakes. One of the most serious was in 1985. It killed thousands of people in the capital, Mexico City, and destroyed large areas of the city.

## Mexico's landscapes

Mexico has many different landscapes. There are deserts in the north, and mountain ranges along the east and west sides of the country. A high plateau is in the center, with rain forests in the south, and many long, sandy beaches.

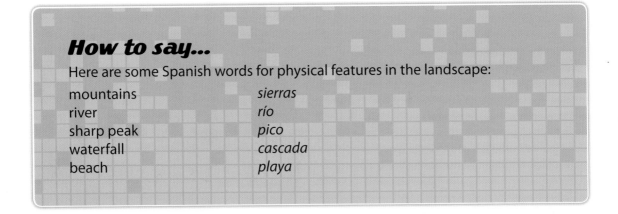

### How to say...

Here are some Spanish words for physical features in the landscape:

| | |
|---|---|
| mountains | *sierras* |
| river | *río* |
| sharp peak | *pico* |
| waterfall | *cascada* |
| beach | *playa* |

This rain forest is in southern Mexico.

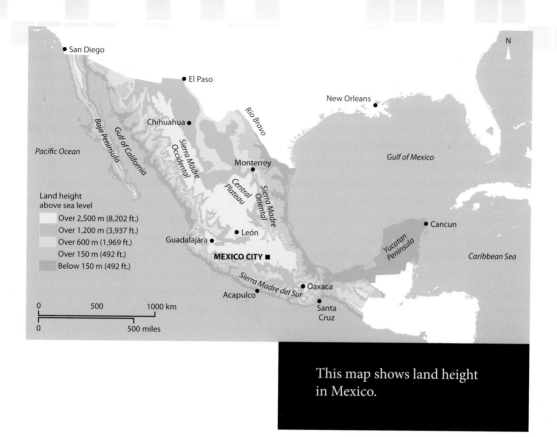

This map shows land height in Mexico.

## The Central Plateau

The Central Plateau is a large area of high, flat land. Mountain ranges, or sierras, are to the west and the east of the plateau. The climate here is **temperate**, neither too hot nor too cold. This is where most Mexicans live.

## From deserts to rain forests

The Sonora Desert straddles the border of Mexico and the United States. This is a desert of thorny shrubs, trees, and cacti. The climate here is hot and dry, with occasional sand storms. It can get very cold at night in the winter. In contrast, in the south there are dense, lush rain forests. Here the climate is warm and humid and it feels hot and sticky all year round.

## Rivers

The most famous and longest river in Mexico is the Rio Bravo, which forms part of the border with the United States, where it is called the Rio Grande. It rises in Colorado and ends in the Gulf of Mexico. Cities and farms use so much of its water that less than 20 percent makes it all the way to the sea.

## Stormy weather

Mexico has regular **hurricanes**, with strong winds and heavy rain. They damage buildings, cause serious flooding, and often cause deaths. Hurricanes happen between June and November. In August 2010, Hurricane Alex killed three people in northern Mexico.

## Daily Life

In the countryside, many people do not own any land and depend on finding work every day. Jobs such as this are usually very badly paid. Many poor workers move to the cities where they live in **shantytowns** in houses made from whatever materials people can find.

Local residents are examining lamp posts knocked down by Hurricane Jimena in Puerto San Carlos in 2009.

# Rich in resources

Mexico's most important natural resource is oil. Selling, or **exporting**, oil to other countries earns Mexico 70 percent of all money it earns from trading. The government of Mexico owns its industry, called PEMEX. It is the second largest oil company in the world.

Mexico is also an important producer of metals. It mines silver, copper, gold, lead, and zinc—all important minerals that have helped Mexico become one of the richest countries in **Latin America**. But only a few Mexicans benefit from this. The majority of Mexicans remain very poor.

# Cash crops

Commercial **plantations** still produce **cash crops**, such as sugar, tobacco, cotton, and coffee, that Mexico sells to other countries. Coffee is a valuable cash crop. Mexico has about 703,341 hectares (1.7 million acres) of coffee-growing land, much of it cleared by cutting down forests. Mexico has given the world a wide range of fruits and vegetables, such as avocados, tomatoes, papayas, pineapples, guava, and vanilla beans. Chocolate is also originally from Mexico.

The Cananea copper mine is one of the largest open pit copper mines in the world.

# Wildlife: Rich in Biodiversity

With over 200,000 different **species**, few places on Earth have as many plants and animal as Mexico. Mexico is home to 707 different reptiles, 438 mammals, and an amazing 26,000 different kinds of plants.

## Life in the desert

The deserts are full of plants and animals that have adapted to the harsh conditions of very high temperatures and a lack of rain. The cactus is probably the most famous. It is able to store moisture in its stem. Mexico has nearly 50 percent of all the cactus species in the world.

Jaguars also live in the mountains of the Sonora Desert. The jaguar is one of Mexico's most endangered animals. Their numbers are falling, but they live in remote areas. This gives them some protection from ranchers and **poachers**. The Aztecs named their bravest fighters "Jaguar Warriors."

The jaguar is one of Mexico's most endangered animals.

This rain forest is being cleared for agriculture.

## Disappearing rain forests

Mexico's rain forests are wonderful places, but are only a third of the size they once were, causing a loss of **biodiversity**. Mexico is second only to Brazil when it comes to destroying forests. Trees have been cut down to create farms for raising beef cattle, for new towns, and for roads. Timber is still one of Mexico's main products. **Deforestation** has threatened the survival of rain forest animals, such as monkeys, cougars, anteaters, and birds, such as the scarlet macaw.

## YOUNG PEOPLE

Young people are becoming more aware of conservation issues and Mexico's precious wildlife. Many go to **eco-tourist** campsites to learn more about nature.

Monarch butterflies sometimes gather on tree trunks in central Mexico.

## The Monarch butterfly

Every year the Monarch butterfly flies up to 4,000 kilometers (2,485 miles) from Canada and the United States to spend the winter in Mexico. Mexico has created special reserves for Monarch butterflies in the Sierra Madre mountain range in the northwest. Thousands gather on special fir trees. People who have seen this say it is one of the wonders of the world.

## Sea life

The seas around Mexico are teeming with wildlife of all kinds. Off the west coast, gray whales swim thousands of miles each year from the cold Bering Sea near Alaska to breed in the warmer seas off Mexico. People often spot marlins, tuna, and seals. In the Gulf of Mexico, there are dolphins and green turtles. But leaks from oil wells, especially an oil spill in April 2010, have damaged some of the wildlife.

## Daily Life

Most Mexican women visit street markets every day to buy fresh fruit and vegetables. Most of the produce is locally grown on small farms, with some tropical fruit transported inland from the coast.

## Mexico's plants

With its different climates and landscapes, Mexico has a wide range of plants and flowers. The poinsettia is native to Mexico. With its bright red leaves, this plant is often used as a seasonal decoration. It is associated with Christmas because of a Mexican legend about a young girl who goes to give an offering in church at Christmas. She can't afford flowers and takes weeds, but when she places the weeds in the church, they change into bright red poinsettias.

This is Mexico's soap tree yucca plant.

# Infrastructure: Unequal Development

The infrastructure of a country is all the systems necessary for people to live and work, such as schools, crime prevention, health care, and transportation. Many of these are organized by the government. In Mexico, there is a problem with high crime rates and police **corruption**.

## Mexico's government

Mexico is a **democratic** nation. This means that everyone over 18 can vote in elections. In fact, voting is compulsory, and people can be fined if they don't vote. Mexico is a **federal republic**, divided into 31 states, and the federal district of Mexico City. Each state governs itself on some matters and also sends representatives to the central parliament. The head of government is the president. Since December 2006, this has been Felipe Calderon. The next presidential election will be in 2012.

Mexico is divided into 31 states and one federal district, all shown here.

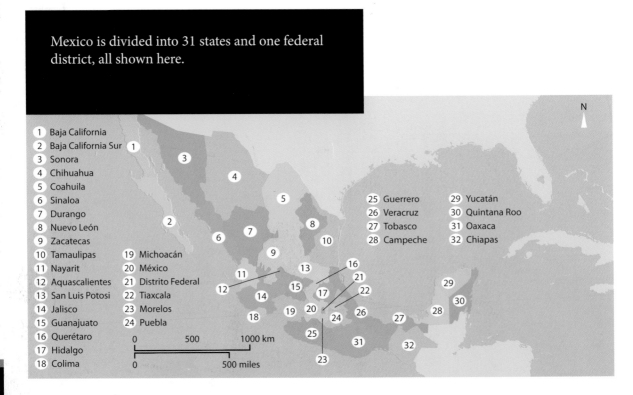

1. Baja California
2. Baja California Sur
3. Sonora
4. Chihuahua
5. Coahuila
6. Sinaloa
7. Durango
8. Nuevo León
9. Zacatecas
10. Tamaulipas
11. Nayarit
12. Aquascalientes
13. San Luis Potosi
14. Jalisco
15. Guanajuato
16. Querétaro
17. Hidalgo
18. Colima
19. Michoacán
20. México
21. Distrito Federal
22. Tiaxcala
23. Morelos
24. Puebla
25. Guerrero
26. Veracruz
27. Tobasco
28. Campeche
29. Yucatán
30. Quintana Roo
31. Oaxaca
32. Chiapas

0    500    1000 km

0    500 miles

N

## Crime

Crime is one of the most important challenges facing Mexico. It has serious problems with **drug trafficking**, including drug gangs fighting each other. There are also problems with illegal smuggling of people into the United States.

Benito Juarez was the first President of Mexico of native descent. This national hero served five times between 1861 and 1872.

## Making and selling

In 1994 Mexico joined the North American Free Trade Agreement (NAFTA). This agreement lifted many of the restrictions and taxes between member countries. It made it easier for Mexico to trade with the United States and Canada. Mexico now sells more than 80 percent of the goods it makes to the United States. It buys 50 percent of its **imports** from the United States. Many new U.S.-owned factories, known as *maquiladoras* in Spanish, have been built along the border. They make goods such as television sets, car parts, electronics, and clothes. The workers in these factories, who are mostly women, are paid less than U.S. workers, so it costs less to produce goods.

## Sending money home

In 2009 Mexicans living abroad sent $21.2 billion back to their families in Mexico. This income is Mexico's second most important source of foreign money after oil.

## CARLOS SLIM (B. 1940)

Carlos Slim was born in Mexico City. In 2010 he was declared to be the world's richest man, ahead of Microsoft's Bill Gates. It is estimated that he is worth $53.5 billion.

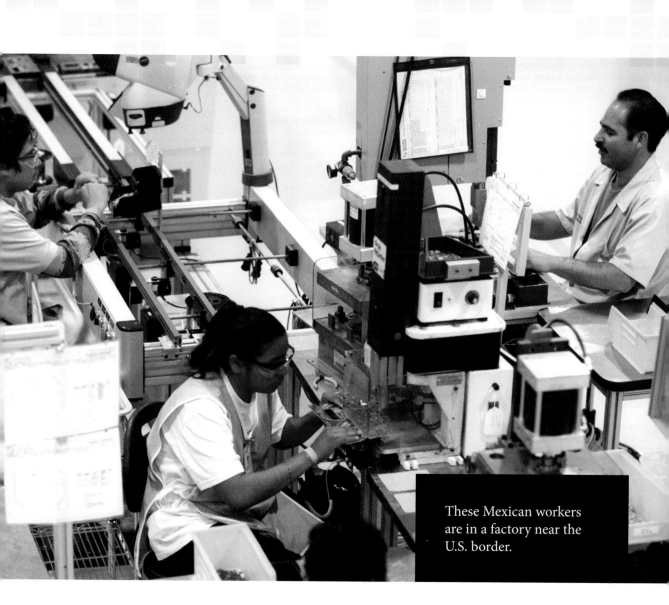

These Mexican workers are in a factory near the U.S. border.

## Health

Americans sometimes come to Mexico for health care because it is good and much less expensive. But it is not free, and the poorest Mexicans cannot afford it. They rely on the government health system.

Swine flu started in Mexico in 2009. The **World Health Organization** declared that a **pandemic** was possible. Mexico closed down all nonessential businesses and other countries limited travel to and from Mexico. Luckily, although swine flu was very dangerous, it was not as serious as first thought.

## Going to school

The Mexican government believes it is very important to improve schools. It has put a lot of money into making sure that there is a place for every child. Primary schools are free, but there are also private schools where parents pay.

Children start school when they are six. The government wants all children to stay in school until they are 16, but some poorer children leave early to help support their families. Schools have improved, and now over 90 percent of Mexicans over 15 can read and write.

### Daily Life

Family is very important in Mexico. As more people become more educated and live in cities, they often choose to have smaller families. People used to have six or seven children, but now two or three is more common.

Preschool and kindergarten education is available for all children between three and five. In Mexico it is known as *jardín de niños* (garden of children).

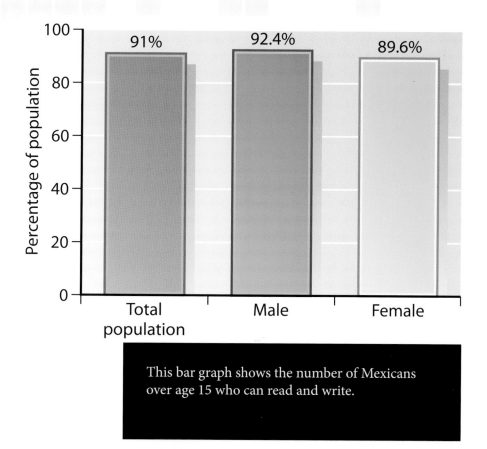

This bar graph shows the number of Mexicans over age 15 who can read and write.

## YOUNG PEOPLE

School starts at 8:00 AM with the singing of the national anthem (see page 38). Children are taught subjects including Spanish, math, history, and English. Pupils get home around 3:00 PM, eat a late lunch, and start their homework and chores.

## Getting around

A cheap and efficient bus service covers Mexico. But traveling long distances takes a long time. People fly if they can afford it. Mexico City and Monterrey have **metro** systems. In Mexico City, this is the best way to get around. Driving across the city through terrible traffic can take at least three hours. It is one of the largest cities in the world, with a population of 18 million.

# Culture: Diverse and Unique

When the Spaniards brought Christianity to Mexico many of the native peoples' beliefs, gods, and **rituals** were absorbed into it. People in Mexico are very religious. Most are Catholics, and there are many festivals to mark special occasions.

## YOUNG PEOPLE

In Mexico girls are often named Maria after the Virgin Mary. Jesus is a common name for boys. To avoid confusion, children are given a middle name, and are often known by this name.

## Fiesta!

As well as Christmas and Easter, Mexicans celebrate *Día de los Muertos* or "Day of the Dead." This holiday, on November 1, honors dead **ancestors**. People dress up in costumes, sometimes to make them look like skeletons. They create **shrines** for dead friends and family, and leave presents on their graves. It is not a sad day, but one of celebration and fun.

Children dress up for the Day of the Dead celebrations.

Traditional Spanish dress is part of Mexican culture along with the costumes and cultures of the native peoples of Mexico.

Mexican Independence Day is celebrated on September 15 and 16. It starts when the president rings a bell and shouts "Long Live Mexico" from the balcony of his palace. There are fireworks, feasts, and parades. In 2010 there were special celebrations for the 200th anniversary of the start of the fight for independence.

## Religions of Mexico

| | |
|---|---|
| Roman Catholic | 76.5% |
| Protestant | 6.3% |
| Other | 0.3% |
| Unspecified | 13.8% |
| None | 3.9% |

## Daily Life

Everywhere you go in Mexico, you see pictures of Our Lady of Guadalupe. The story is that an image of the Virgin Mary miraculously appeared on a peasant's cloak while he was working in fields near the town of Guadalupe. People pray to her image when they are worried.

## A healthy diet?

Mexican food has strong flavors, and is spicy and colorful. Mexican flat bread is called tortilla. Tortillas are made from **corn meal** in central and southern Mexico and flour in northern Mexico. A typical lunch would be tortillas wrapped around chicken and cheese. People sometimes use tortillas instead of using a fork or spoon. Evening meals are usually something more substantial, such as stews of pork, chicken, or beef. Eggs are served with refried beans (see recipe right) and tortillas with avocados, cheese, and vegetables.

Refried beans with a tortilla is a tasty Mexican meal.

The traditional Mexican diet is very healthy. But as Mexicans become wealthier, they are influenced more by a Western lifestyle, including fast food. Mexico is beginning to get problems such as childhood **obesity**. In 2010 the government banned fried foods and candy from schools to help solve this problem.

## Refried beans with tortilla

Refried beans are a common meal in Mexico. Be sure to have an adult help you make this delicious recipe.

Ingredients

- 1 can of refried beans
- 1 cup of prepared **salsa**
- 1 chopped green chilli
- 2 cups of shredded cheddar or Monterey jack cheese
- ½ cup sliced black olives
- 8 flour tortillas or taco shells
- shredded lettuce, sour cream, and chopped tomato

Method

Place the refried beans, salsa, and green chilli in a saucepan and turn the heat to medium. Bring the mixture to the boil. While you are doing this, heat the tortillas in the oven or microwave until they are warm. When the beans are really hot, add the cheese and black olives and stir well. When the cheese has melted, put the mixture on the tortillas (or in the taco shells), and top with the lettuce, sour cream, and tomato.

Make sure that an adult is present to help whenever you are using a knife or cooking food.

## Popular sports

Soccer, or *fútbol* as it is called in Spanish, is the most popular sport in Mexico. It is played in stadiums, on fields or open ground, or on the streets. Mexico reached the second round in the 2010 World Cup Finals in South Africa.

Another national sport is *charreria*, a series of horse riding events. It's similar to rodeos in the United States. Bullfighting, which the Spanish brought to Mexico, is also very popular. Although it is a much-loved sport, animal rights organizations campaign against its cruelty. Wrestling, boxing, and basketball are other popular sports.

## Music and art

Music in Mexico has been influenced by different cultures. Although young people enjoy hip-hop and rock music, traditional Mexican music is still popular with all age groups. Like music, the different peoples and cultures of Mexico influence the art of Mexico. The Mayans and Aztecs produced clay pots and brightly colored embroidery and baskets. These are still made today. With its many historic buildings and ruins, Mexico has 29 **UNESCO World Heritage sites**—more than any other country in the Americas.

### FRIDA KAHLO (1907–1954)

Frida Kahlo was an important Mexican painter. Her pictures are full of color and use a number of the art traditions of the Mayans and Aztecs. Many of her paintings were self-portraits. Kahlo was married to the famous Mexican painter Diego Rivera.

A feature of Mexican children's parties is often the piñata. It is a hollow, papier-maché shape, such as a donkey, filled with candy and small toys. Children take turns hitting the piñata with a stick until it breaks and the toys and candy fall out.

## Daily Life

Mariachi bands are everywhere in Mexico. These musicians walk around as they play in the streets or in restaurants. They wear silver-studded charro outfits, like cowboy clothes, and wide-brimmed hats. They play violins, trumpets, and guitars. These are instruments introduced by the Spanish, but mariachi music has its roots in all the different Mexican cultures.

# Mexico Today

Mexico is a country with many problems and, at the same time, great possibilities for development.

To improve life for all its people, Mexico must tackle certain problems. One of the most important is the huge difference between the few wealthy people and the majority who are still very poor. In the past, this has caused unrest and it could again.

Mexico must also tackle its crime rate. The murder rate is very high. With more than 20 million visitors a year, tourism is vitally important to Mexico. Although now the violence is mainly restricted to drug gangs, many tourists have recently decided not to go to Mexico because of news reports of violence and murders.

## Fast-growing economy

Mexico has one of the fastest-growing economies in the world. It is rich in natural resources, but past government failings have kept its wealth from being shared among the people. The cities may have modern offices, shopping malls, and apartment buildings, but they are surrounded by **shantytowns** and poor rural villages full of old people and young children.

## The future

Despite the problems that Mexico faces, it is an exciting and lively country that has good prospects and hope for the future.

## ELLEN OCHOA (B. 1958)

Ellen Ochoa, who is half Mexican, became the first **Hispanic** female astronaut when she flew for nine days on board the shuttle *Discovery* in 1993. She flew again on *Atlantis* in 2002.

Young Mexicans are growing up in a rapidly changing country.

# Fact File

**Official Title**: The United Mexican States (Estados Unidos Mexicanos)

**Area**: 1.9 million square kilometers (733,594 square miles)

**Population**: 111,211,789

**Ethnic Groups**: Mestizos 60%, Native Americans 30%, European (mainly of Spanish origin) 10%

**Capital City**: Mexico City

**Some Other Large Cities**: Guadalajara, Puebla, Monterrey

**Mexico's Coastline**: 9,339 kilometers (5,798 miles)

**Official Language**: Spanish

**Other Languages**: Mayan, Nahuatl, and more than 60 others

**National Holiday**: Independence Day (September 15)

**Money**: The peso. There are 100 centavos in 1 peso.

**Cell Phones**: 79.4 million (2009)

**Highest Point**: Pico de Orizaba at 5,636 m (18,490 ft.) above

**Lowest Point**: Laguna Salada at -10 m (33 ft.) below sea level

This young man has decorated his swine flu mask for fun.

Mexico has the 11th largest population in the world.

More than 12 percent of the U.S. population is made up of people of Mexican descent.

Mexico is a member of many international organizations including the **World Health Organization**, The World Trade Organization, and the International Labor Organization.

Mexico City hosted the Olympic Games in 1968.

The border between Mexico and the United States is about 3,218 kilometers (2,000 miles) long. It is the second longest in the world, after the U.S.-Canada border.

## The Mexican National Anthem

A poet called Francisco González Bocanegra wrote the words to the Mexican national anthem in the mid-1800s. The words reflect how Mexicans have had to fight for their independence and freedom:

> *Mexicans, at the cry of war*
> *Make ready your sword and horse,*
> *Let the core of your land resound*
> *To the sonorous roar of the cannon*
> *Fatherland! Be crowned with the olive branch*
> *Of peace by the divine archangel*
> *For in heaven your eternal destiny*
> *Was written by the finger of God.*
> *But if a foreign enemy dares*
> *To profane your land with his foot,*
> *Remember, dear Fatherland,*
> *That Heaven*
> *Has given you a soldier in each son.*

Puerto Vallarta, Mexico, sits
along the Pacific Ocean.

# Timeline

BCE means "before the common era." When this appears after a date, it refers to the number of years before the Christian religion began. BCE dates are always counted backward.

CE means "common era." When this appears after a date, it refers to the time after the Christian religion began.

## BCE

| | |
|---|---|
| 1500 | The beginnings of the Mayan civilization |
| 1200–900 | The Olmec civilization builds huge structures |

## CE

| | |
|---|---|
| 300–900 | The Mayan culture and civilization is at its peak |
| 1325-1521 | The Aztecs flourish, and establish Tenochtitlán as their capital |
| 1519–1521 | Hernán Cortés and the Spanish conquistadors invade and conquer Mexico |
| 1523–1821 | Spain rules Mexico |
| 1810–1821 | Mexico fights Spain for its independence and eventually wins in 1821 |
| 1821 | Mexico becomes independent |
| 1845 | Mexico loses Texas to the United States |
| 1910–1911 | The people of Mexico rebel against their rulers and overthrow the dictator Porfirio Diaz |
| 1917 | A new constitution is adopted granting more rights for poor people and ensuring that Mexico always remains a democracy |
| 1942 | Mexico declares war on Japan and Germany |

| 1960 | There is civil unrest as people protest about the big differences between the rich and poor in Mexico |
| 1968 | Mexico City hosts the Olympic Games |
| 1976 | Huge offshore oil reserves are discovered |
| 1985 | Nearly 10,000 people are killed in an earthquake in Mexico City |
| 1993 | Mexico joins the North American Free Trade Agreement (NAFTA), making it easier to trade with the United States and Canada |
| 2000 | Vicente Fox Quesada of the PAN party wins the presidential election |
| 2006 | Felipe Calderon wins the presidential election |
| 2007 | Heavy rains flood nearly the entire southern state of Tabasco. Some 500,000 people are made homeless in one of the country's worst natural disasters. |
| 2009 | One of Mexico's most wanted drug lords is killed in a shootout with state security forces |
| 2010 | U.S. President Barack Obama signs into law a bill to put even more deterrents along the Mexican border to stop the flow of illegal immigrants |

# Glossary

**active** describes a volcano that is still capable of erupting

**ally** friend or supporter

**ancestor** person from whom someone is descended, for example a great-grandparent

**biodiversity** many different kinds of plants and animals

**cash crop** crop produced to be sold, usually to another country

**civil war** war between two groups of people in the same country

**civilization** advanced society

**colony** country ruled by another country

**conquistador** 16th-century Spanish soldier

**corn meal** flour made from ground corn (maize)

**corruption** immoral or unlawful action

**deforestation** destruction of forests, especially rain forests, to make room for farms and buildings

**democracy** system where people vote for who they want to rule them

**dictator** ruler with absolute power who has not been elected

**drug trafficking** buying and selling illegal drugs

**eco-tourist** traveler who does not damage the land being visited

**export** goods sold to another country

**extinct** no longer exists

**federal republic** country made up of states

**Hispanic** someone from the American continent whose first language is Spanish

**hurricane** severe tropical storm

**import** buy goods from a foreign country

**land redistribution** sharing out land more equally

**Latin America** countries of North and South America south of the United States

**mestizo**  person of mixed European and Native American descent

**metro**  underground railway system

**obesity**  dangerously overweight

**pandemic**  disease once it has spread over a wide geographic area

**peninsula**  area of land that juts out into the water from the main land

**plantation**  large farm where crops are grown

**plateau**  area of high, flat land

**poacher**  someone who hunts or fishes illegally

**ritual**  ceremony or tradition

**salsa**  spicy sauce of chopped tomatoes, onions, chilli peppers, and herbs

**shantytown**  slum settlement on the edge of a city

**shrine**  place devoted to a holy person or god where prayers are said

**species**  group of animals or plants that have certain characteristics in common

**tectonic plate**  segment of Earth's crust

**temperate**  neither too hot nor too cold

**Tropic of Cancer**  line of latitude 23° north of the Equator

**tsunami**  giant wave often caused by an earthquake or volcano under the sea

**typhus**  deadly infectious disease

**UNESCO World Heritage site**  place such as a building, forest, or monument that is considered to be of great value to the world and is listed as such by the United Nations Educational, Scientific and Cultural Organization

**World Health Organization**  agency body of the United Nations that works to improve and promote world health

# Find Out More

## Books

Berg, Elizabeth. *Festivals of the World: Mexico*. Tarrytown, NY: Benchmark Books, 2010.

Gagne, Tammy. *Your Land and My Land: We Visit Mexico*. Hockessin, Del,: Mitchell Lane, 2010.

Jermyn, Leslie and Fiona Conboy. *Welcome to My Country: Mexico*. Tarrytown, N.Y.: Benchmark Books, 2010.

Kalman, Bobbie and Niki Walker. *Spotlight on Mexico*. New York: Crabtree Publishing, 2008.

Krebs, Laurie. *Off We Go to Mexico*. Cambridge, Mass.: Barefoot Books, 2006.

Laundau, Elaine. *Mexico*. Danbury, Conn.: New True Books, 2008.

McCulloch, Julie. *World of Recipes: Mexico*. Chicago: Heinemann Library, 2009.

Sexton, Colleen. *Exploring Countries*: Mexico. Minneapolis: Bellwether Media, 2011.

Streissguth, Tom. *Country Explorer: Mexico*. Minneapolis: Lerner, 2008.

## Websites

http://tides.sfasu.edu/Teachers/Tides/docs/VirtualExpeditions/virtualexpeditions.html
This website includes three useful videos on different aspects of Mexican life.

http://aztecs.mrdonn.org/index.html
This site has lots of information about the Aztecs.

# Places to visit

Chichen Itza
See this ancient Mayan city in the Mexican state of Yucatan.

Mexico City
Mexico City is one of largest cities in the world with ancient Aztec ruins.

Palenque
See ancient Mayan temples rising out of the jungle.

Santa Prisca y San Sebastián Church
One of Mexico's most impressive churches is located in Taxco.

Teotihuacán
This ancient city includes the Avenue of the Dead, the Pyramid of the Sun, and the Pyramid of the Moon.

# Topic Tools

You can use these topic tools for your school projects. Trace the flag and map on to a sheet of paper, using the thick black outlines to guide you, then color in your pictures. Make sure you use the right colors for the flag!

The flag of Mexico shows an eagle eating a serpent, sitting on a cactus in a lake. These symbols come from an Aztec legend. The colors of the flag are green, white, and red. The green stands for independence and the white stands for purity. The red stands for the national heroes who died fighting for Mexico's independence.

N

Mexico City

# Index

## Titles in the series